D1109902

The Bathroom Football Book

By Jack Kreismer

RED-LETTER PRESS, INC.
SADDLE RIVER, NEW JERSEY

Introduction and Acknowledgement

The Bathroom Football Book is intended for all those who have a passing interest in the game.

The trivia and puzzlers throughout the book will challenge the wits of the hardcore fan. At the same time, bathroom-reading browsers will enjoy flipping through the pages for "potluck" - and everyone will enjoy the privy-related pigskin material.

A roll call to the following who've huddled on this book and whose efforts continue to keep The Bathroom Library (see back page) on the publishing throne:

Cyndi Bellerose
Angela Demers
Glenn Fraller
Robin Kreismer
Sylvia Martin
Geoff Scowcroft

Yours flushingly,
Jack Kreismer

First And Ten

1. What NFL player spent the most seasons with one club?

2. Name the only team to be held without a touchdown in a Super Bowl game.

3. Two of the Chicago Bears' 1965 first round draft selections are members of the Pro Football Hall of Fame. Do you know them?

4. Who was the first black player to win the Heisman Trophy?

5. What is the name of the trophy awarded to the Canadian Football League champ?

6. Who was the last coach of the Baltimore Colts?

7. Jake Gibbs was a catcher for the New York Yankees from 1962 to 1971. He was also a consensus All-American quarterback in 1960. For what college team?

8. Who were the three men behind the mike for ABC's first Monday Night Football game?

9. Who passed for more yards than anyone in AFL history?

10. Who was the Clemson player punched by Ohio State coach Woody Hayes in the 1978 Gator Bowl?

1. *Jim Marshall, 19 seasons with the Minnesota Vikings.*

2. *Miami which lost 24-3 to Dallas in Super Bowl VI.*

3. *Gale Sayers and Dick Butkus.*

4. *Ernie Davis.*

5. *The Grey Cup.*

6. *Frank Kush.*

7. *Mississippi.*

8. *Keith Jackson, Howard Cosell and Don Meredith.*

9. *Jack Kemp (21,130 yards from 1960 to 1969).*

10. *Charlie Bauman.*

Passing Fads

Listed below are the last names of famous passing-receiving combos. The letters are in their proper order, but the names have been combined. See if you can *flush* out the quarterback and the receiver.

Example— FJOOUINTERS = Fouts and Joiner.

1. TSITHOTFLNEER

2. BSWRAADSNHANW

3. UBERNIRTYAS

4. MDUAPREIRNO

5. MROINTCANEA

6. LBAIMLEOTNNNICIKOFAF

7. SPTEAAURBSAOCNH

8. DATAWYSLOONR

9. SDTOAWLRERR

10. CUQNUNINIGHCAMK

1.   *Tittle and Shofner.*

2.   *Bradshaw and Swann.*

3.   *Unitas and Berry.*

4.   *Marino and Duper.*

5.   *Montana and Rice.*

6.   *Lamonica and Biletnikoff.*

7.   *Staubach and Pearson.*

8.   *Dawson and Taylor.*

9.   *Starr and Dowler.*

10.   *Cunningham and Quick.*

Thoughts of the Throne

"Supposedly, he weighs 325. Hey, who knows? He's running twice a day - from the refrigerator to the bathroom."

—Chicago Bears coach Mike Ditka on
the off-season conditioning of
William "The Refrigerator" Perry

Pigskin Potpourri

1. What is the most popular nickname for college football teams?

2. Can you name the original Fearsome Foursome defensive line of the Los Angeles Rams?

3. Do you know the most lopsided score in college football history?

4. What number did Red Grange wear?

5. Former NFL wide receiver Bobby Moore is better known as. . .?

6. Name the NFL team which drafted Joe Namath.

7. Who holds the NFL record for most seasons with 1,000 or more yards rushing?

8. What NFL team has two home stadiums?

9. Who was the founder of the defunct Chicago College All-Star Game (a contest which pitted collegiate stars against the NFL champion)? Hint: he also founded baseball's All-Star Game.

10. What Super Bowl saw the smallest crowd in the game's history?

1.   *Tigers (7 major schools, 28 in all).*

2.   *Merlin Olsen, Deacon Jones, Roosevelt Grier and Lamar Lundy.*

3.   *Georgia Tech shut out Cumberland (Tennessee), 222-0 in 1916.*

4.   *77.*

5.   *Ahmad Rashad.*

6.   *The St. Louis Cardinals.*

7.   *Walter Payton (10).*

8.   *The Packers who play at Lambeau Field in Green Bay and at County Stadium in Milwaukee.*

9.   *Arch Ward.*

10.   *Super Bowl I. A turnout of 61,946 fans witnessed the Packers beat the Chiefs at the Los Angeles Memorial Coliseum.*

Thoughts of the Throne

Gerald Ford, an all-Big Ten center during his school days, received a toilet seat with the seal of the University of Michigan displayed on it. While he was president, Ford reportedly liked the seat so much he had it installed in the White House.

X's and O's

Fill in the blanks based on the clues provided. We've already filled in those spaces which contain x's and o's.

1. _ _ O _ _ _ X   A Chicago club until 1960.

2. _ _ _ _   _ O X   Holds NFL consecutive game scoring record — 151.

3. _ _ _ _ O _   "Famous" Ohio town.

4. _ _ _ _ _ _ _   _ _ X _ _ _ _ _   Kicked longest NCAA field goal.

5. _ _ _ _ _ _ O _'_   _ _ _   Namath nightspot.

6. X _ _   Niners first Super Bowl win.

7. _ O _   _ _ _ _ _ _ O   Navy Heisman winner.

8. _ X _ _ _   _ O _ _ _   Wersching never missed one in '84.

9. _ _ _   _ _ O _ _ _   First NFL prez.

10. _ O _   _ _ X   USC tackle, #1 draft pick of Colts in 1960.

1. *Phoenix.*

2. *Fred Cox.*

3. *Canton.*

4. *Russell Erxleben.*

5. *Bachelor's III.*

6. *XVI.*

7. *Joe Bellino.*

8. *Extra point.*

9. *Jim Thorpe.*

10. *Ron Mix.*

Thoughts of the Throne

Florida State football coach Bobby Bowden spoke of a recruiting trip he once took on a small plane that flew into a storm. According to the coach, the pilot noticed how scared Bowden was, and in an attempt to ease his worries, said, "Do you realize that more accidents happen in the bathrooms of homes than in airplanes?"

Bowden responded, "Now, I'm afraid to go to the bathroom."

Screen Test

1. Who wrote "Paper Lion?"

2. Who played the author in the above movie?

3. What was the name of the television movie about Brian Piccolo?

4. What actor played the title role in "Jim Thorpe, All American?"

5. Who played Spearchucker Jones in the movie "M*A*S*H?"

6. Jennifer Edwards played the title role in what TV show that interrupted a football game?

7. Name the "Hill Street Blues" star who was the 1971 Heisman runnerup and later a pro running back.

8. What Florida State running back starred in "The Longest Yard?"

9. Do you know the former Colt lineman who starred in the "Police Academy" comedy films?

10. In the TV sitcom "Webster," who played Webster's father?

1.   *George Plimpton.*

2.   *Alan Alda.*

3.   *"Brian's Song."*

4.   *Burt Lancaster.*

5.   *Former Kansas City Chiefs defensive back Fred Williamson.*

6.   *"Heidi."*

7.   *Ed Marinaro.*

8.   *Burt Reynolds.*

9.   *Bubba Smith.*

10.   *Alex Karras.*

Alma Mater

Match the player with the college he attended.

1.	Johnny Unitas	A.	Louisiana Tech
2.	Herschel Walker	B.	South Carolina
3.	John Elway	C.	Purdue
4.	George Rogers	D.	Virginia Tech
5.	Paul Hornung	E.	Texas
6.	Jim Everett	F.	Georgia
7.	Lawrence Taylor	G.	Louisville
8.	Terry Bradshaw	H.	Notre Dame
9.	Bruce Smith	I.	Stanford
10.	Earl Campbell	J.	North Carolina

1. *G.*

2. *F.*

3. *I.*

4. *B.*

5. *H.*

6. *C.*

7. *J.*

8. *A.*

9. *D.*

10. *E.*

Thoughts of the Throne

Just before Super Bowl XXI (Giants versus Broncos), Harvey Schultz, commissioner of the New York City Department of Environmental Protection, issued a "bowl warning." Schultz suggested that Super Bowl viewers should can, or at least curb, their trips to the john so the city's water system wouldn't be under too much pressure. A Big Apple p.r. person admitted later that the warning was nothing more than a media prank.

7

Phrase Craze

See if you can figure out what gridiron phrases these items represent.

1. L A R E T A L

2. 

3. MOTION
backfield

4.

```
t   t
h   h
g   g
i   i
r   r
```

5. reverse
reverse

1. *Backward lateral.*

2. *Halftime.*

3. *Backfield in motion.*

4. *Uprights.*

5. *Double reverse.*

Thoughts of the Throne

Toilet seats proved to be a popular commode-ity in Denver when the Broncos won the AFC title in 1977. The city's fans developed an "Orange Crush" on their team, many of whom sent orange colored toilet seats to Denver's head coach, Red Miller.

Take Me Out To The Old Ball Park

Name the pro team(s) that used to play in these stadiums.

1. Kezar Stadium.

2. Wrigley Field.

3. Metropolitan Stadium.

4. War Memorial Stadium.

5. Briggs Stadium.

6. Franklin Field.

7. Balboa Stadium.

8. Nippert Stadium.

9. Comiskey Park.

10. Griffith Stadium.

Answers

1. *San Francisco 49ers and Oakland Raiders.*

2. *Chicago Bears.*

3. *Minnesota Vikings.*

4. *Buffalo Bills.*

5. *Detroit Lions.*

6. *Philadelphia Eagles.*

7. *San Diego Chargers.*

8. *Cincinnati Bengals.*

9. *Chicago Cardinals.*

10. *Washington Redskins.*

Quote Unquote

"Old quarterbacks never die, they just drop back and. . ."

Your job is to finish the quote by answering the following clues and then writing the boxed letter in the corresponding space at the bottom of the page. (Hint: they are all quarterbacks' names.) We've started you off with the first one.

1. A former General   <u>S</u> <u>I</u> <u>(P)</u> <u>E</u>

2. High-topped hoofer   _ _ _ _ (_) _

3. The Polish Rifle   _ _ _ _ _ (_) _ _

4. His center was Ringo.   (_) _ _ _ _
    He is. . .

5. Canadian Prime Minister? _ _ _ _ _ (_) _

6. Jo Jo's ex-mate   _ _ _ _ _ _ _ (_)

7. Sir Francis   _ (_) _ _ _ _ _ _ _

8. Jet in the wings   _ (_) _ _

$$\frac{P}{1} \ \frac{}{2} \ \frac{}{3} \ \frac{}{4} \quad \frac{}{5} \ \frac{}{6} \ \frac{}{7} \ \frac{}{8}$$

1. *Sipe.*

2. *Unitas.*

3. *Jaworski.*

4. *Starr.*

5. *Trudeau.*

6. *Bradshaw.*

7. *Tarkenton.*

8. *Ryan.*

<u>P</u> <u>A</u> <u>S</u> <u>S</u>   <u>A</u> <u>W</u> <u>A</u> <u>Y</u>

Pigskin Potpourri

1. What colleges were known as the Big Three before the Ivy League was created?

2. To the nearest inch, how long is a football?

3. Rollen Stewart, a born again Christian, has made it his mission to spread the word by displaying what banner often seen at football stadiums?

4. Do more NFL teams play their home games on natural or artificial turf?

5. How long is a team timeout in the final two minutes of each half in a pro game?

6. What college football star was the father-in-law of the late singer Rick Nelson?

7. Who did the Dallas Texans become?

8. Fran Tarkenton has thrown for more pass completions in his career than any other quarterback. Who is second?

9. Where is the College Football Hall of Fame?

10. Including city names and team names, what are the only two letters not used in the spelling of any of the NFL clubs?

1.   *Harvard, Yale and Princeton.*

2.   *Eleven inches.*

3.   *"JOHN 3:16."*

4.   *Artificial (15 to 13).*

5.   *40 seconds.*

6.   *Tom Harmon.*

7.   *The Kansas City Chiefs.*

8.   *Dan Fouts.*

9.   *Kings Mill, Ohio.*

10.   *Q and Z.*

Initially Speaking

In this quiz, the football related number on the left is based upon the first letters for words which we've provided on the right.

Example: 10 = Y. for a F.D.   (Yards for a First Down)

1.   4 = Q. in a G.

2.   28 = T. in P.F.

3.   900 = S. in a Q.

4.   4 = T. in the C.D. of the A.F.C.

5.   3 = T.O. per T. in a H.

6.   360 = F. on a F.F. (I. the E.Z.)

7.   16,726 = Y.G. by W.P.

8.   6 = P. for a T.

9.   11 = P. on a T.

10.   16 = G. in a R.S. in the N.F.L.

1.   *4 = Quarters in a Game.*

2.   *28 = Teams in Pro Football.*

3.   *900 = Seconds in a Quarter.*

4.   *4 = Teams in the Central Division of the American Football Conference.*

5.   *3 = Time Outs per Team in a Half.*

6.   *360 = Feet on a Football Field (Including the End Zone).*

7.   *16,726 = Yards Gained by Walter Payton.*

8.   *6 = Points for a Touchdown.*

9.   *11 = Players on a Team.*

10.   *16 = Games in a Regular Season in the National Football League.*

T - Formation

The answers to these questions are all players whose last names begin with the letter "T."

1. They called him "The Assassin."

2. A first round draft pick from Wisconsin, he's been a perennial Pro Bowl receiver since his rookie year in '85.

3. A broken leg busted up this quarterback's career.

4. This quarterback and his team lost to Penn State in the Fiesta Bowl for the NCAA Championship.

5. He was the first player in either the AFL or NFL to catch 100 passes in a season.

6. He was the "Throwin' Samoan."

7. He punted a record 15 times for the Eagles in a 1987 overtime against the Giants.

8. His 240 straight games played in the NFL is second only to Jim Marshall's 282.

9. He was the first black player to be elected to the Pro Football Hall of Fame.

10. He was traded to the Giants in the early 60's for little known guard Lou Cordileone.

1.   *Jack Tatum.*

2.   *Al Toon.*

3.   *Joe Theismann.*

4.   *Vinny Testaverde.*

5.   *Lionel Taylor.*

6.   *Jack Thompson.*

7.   *John Teltschik.*

8.   *Mick Tingelhoff.*

9.   *Emlen Tunnell.*

10.   *Y.A. Tittle.*

Who Said It?

1. "Nowadays all kids think about is money. When I was a kid all I thought about was eatin'."

2. "Although I never played football, I made many contributions. I went to the University of Southern California in the late 1940s and took the English exams for all the Trojan linemen."

3. "If I drop dead tomorrow, at least I'll know I died in good health."

4. "A real executive goes around with a worried look on his assistants."

5. "I never graduated from Iowa. I was only there for two terms— Truman's and Eisenhower's."

6. "Pro football gave me a good sense of perspective to enter politics. I'd already been booed, cheered, cut, sold, traded and hung in effigy."

7. "An aetheist is a guy who watches a Notre Dame— S.M.U. football game and doesn't care who wins."

8. Old placekickers never die. They just go on missing the point."

9. "To pronounce my name you take 'par' as in golf, 'seag' as in Seagram's whiskey, and 'yen' as in Japanese money. Just think of a drunken Japanese golfer."

10. "A tie is like kissing your sister."

1.   *William "Refrigerator" Perry.*

2.   *Art Buchwald.*

3.   *Bum Phillips.*

4.   *Vince Lombardi.*

5.   *Alex Karras.*

6.   *Jack Kemp.*

7.   *Dwight D. Eisenhower.*

8.   *Lou Groza.*

9.   *Ara Parseghian.*

10.   *Paul "Bear" Bryant.*

Thoughts of the Throne

Name the two NFL teams which once played their home games in Flushing.

The Giants and Jets. Shea Stadium is located in Flushing, a section of Queens which is one of the five boroughs of New York City.

The Hall Of Names

Do you know the first names of these footballers?

1.   Doc Blanchard.

2.   Night Train Lane.

3.   Rocky Bleier.

4.   Weeb Ewbank.

5.   Crazy Legs Hirsch.

6.   Big Daddy Lipscomb.

7.   Spider Lockhart.

8.   Mercury Morris.

9.   Bart Starr.

10. Buddy Ryan.

1.   *Felix.*

2.   *Dick.*

3.   *Robert.*

4.   *Wilber.*

5.   *Elroy.*

6.   *Gene.*

7.   *Carl.*

8.   *Eugene.*

9.   *Bryan.*

10. *James.*

Pigskin Potpourri

1. What is the score of a forfeited college football game?

2. What was the last team Vince Lombardi coached?

3. Technically speaking, what is the shape of a football?

4. The 1972 Miami Dolphins went 17-0 for the best seasonal record in NFL history. The 1986 Chicago Bears, in 19 games, would have had an unblemished record had they not been defeated by what team?

5. What one-time Jets executive was at one time an agent for actor Ronald Reagan?

6. Who was the first college player to gain 6,000 yards rushing?

7. What is the oldest college bowl game?

8. How many time outs is a team allowed in a game?

9. If Pro Football's Hall of Famers were listed alphabetically, whose name would come first?

10. How many NFL teams have bird nicknames?

Answers

1. *1-0.*

2. *The Washington Redskins.*

3. *It is a prolate spheroid.*

4. *Miami.*

5. *Sonny Werblin.*

6. *Tony Dorsett.*

7. *The Rose Bowl.*

8. *Six (three per half).*

9. *Herb Adderley's.*

10. *Four (the Falcons, Cardinals, Eagles and Seahawks).*

True or False

1. During World War II, the depleted rosters of the Eagles and Steelers combined to form one team called the Steagles.

2. In 1980, NBC presented an announcerless telecast of a Jets-Dolphins game.

3. Former Minnesota Vikings placekicker Fred Cox invented the Nerf Ball.

4. George "Papa Bear" Halas played rightfield for the New York Yankees before Babe Ruth.

5. Joe Theismann's name was pronounced "THEES-man" but was changed so that it would rhyme with Heisman (as in the trophy).

6. Giants coach Bill Parcells' first name is Duane.

7. Princeton quarterback Edgar Allan Poe was named to the first All-American football team in 1889.

8. On a cold November day in Pullman, Washington, in 1955, Washington State played San Jose State before a paid crowd of one.

9. The Salad Bowl was played in Phoenix, Arizona, from 1948 to 1952.

10. When the Rose Bowl was first opened, it had no rest rooms and became humorously referred to as the "toilet(less)bowl."

With the rather obvious exception of number ten, all of the statements are true.

A Man For All Seasons

1. What former 49ers running back was the only man to pinch-hit for baseball great Ted Williams?

2. Who's the only man to coach an NFL team and manage a Major League baseball club?

3. Name the man who was an NFL halfback, a pro basketball coach and a Major League baseball umpire.

4. What former NFL player and coach was a pro basketball player with the NBA's Minneapolis Lakers in 1950-51?

5. Who's the only man in the Pro Football Hall of Fame, the College Football Hall of Fame and the Baseball Hall of Fame?

6. A tackle from Syracuse, he was drafted by the Lions in 1959, but became a Major League baseball umpire after a knee injury curtailed his gridiron career. Who is he?

7. What member of the Pro Football Hall of Fame was also a pitcher who gave up two homers to Babe Ruth the year he hit 60 in 1927?

8. Who is the only man to win an Olympic Gold Medal, play in a World Series, and be elected to the Pro Football Hall of Fame?

9. What NBA All-Pro was beaten out for wide receiver on the Cleveland Browns by another All-Pro, Gary Collins?

10. Name the former NFL defensive end who fought an eight round exhibition match against Muhammad Ali.

1.   *Carroll Hardy.*

2.   *Hugo Bezdek who managed the Pittsburgh Pirates from 1917 to 1919 and coached the Cleveland Rams in 1937 and 1938.*

3.   *Hank Soar. He played for the football Giants from 1937 to 1944 and also in 1946, coached basketball's Providence Steamrollers in 1947 and 1948, and was an American League umpire from 1950 to 1971.*

4.   *Bud Grant.*

5.   *Cal Hubbard.*

6.   *Ron Luciano.*

7.   *Ernie Nevers.*

8.   *Jim Thorpe.*

9.   *John Havlicek.*

10.   *Lyle Alzado.*

Broaching Coaching

1. The New York Jets were the first American Football League team to win a Super Bowl, 16-7 over the Colts in 1969. Who was their head coach?

2. Who was the Vikings first coach when they entered the NFL in 1961?

3. How many colleges victories did Paul "Bear" Bryant have?

4. George Halas won more games than any other NFL coach, 325. Who is second on the career victory list?

5. What nickname was given to Miami of Ohio because of the future success of its coaches like Woody Hayes, Bo Schembechler, and Sid Gillman?

6. Which quarterback was not an NFL head coach?

    a) Bart Starr
    b) Bob Waterfield
    c) Charlie Conerly
    d) Otto Graham

7. Who was the first head coach of the Tampa Bay Buccaneers?

8. Of NFL coaches with 100 victories or more, who has the best winning percentage in the league's history?

9. He was the head coach for Heisman Trophy winners at two different schools— Oregon State's Terry Baker in 1962 and UCLA's Gary Beban in 1967. Name him.

10. Who were the coaches for Super Bowl I?

1.   *Weeb Ewbank.*

2.   *Norm Van Brocklin.*

3.   *323.*

4.   *Don Shula.*

5.   *Cradle of Coaches.*

6.   *B.*

7.   *John McKay.*

8.   *John Madden, .763 (103-32-7).*

9.   *Tommy Prothro.*

10.   *Vince Lombardi (Green Bay) and Hank Stram (Kansas City).*

NAMES AND NUMBERS

Listed here are names of players who've had jerseys retired by their respective clubs. What were their numbers?

1.   Walter Payton, Bears

2.   Merlin Olsen, Rams

3.   Floyd Little, Broncos

4.   Lenny Moore, Colts

5.   Len Dawson, Chiefs

6.   Ray Nitschke, Packers

7.   Larry Wilson, Cardinals

8.   Joe Morrison, Giants

9.   Pete Retzlaff, Eagles

10.   John Brodie, 49ers

1. 34.

2. 74.

3. 44.

4. 24.

5. 16.

6. 66.

7. 8.

8. 40.

9. 44.

10. 12.

Thoughts of the Throne

What bathroom-related activity did superstitious Giants running back Alex Webster refuse to do on game day?

Shave.

QUOTE UNQUOTE

"One day you are drinking the wine, and the next day you are picking..."

To complete the above quote by Lou Holtz on the perils of coaching, fill in the spaces based on the clues provided and then insert the boxed letters in the corresponding blanks below. Hint: Each of the answers is the last name of a head coach.

1. Sooner in '73, See ya' later __ __ __ (__) __ __ __
   in '89

2. Papa Bear   (__) __ __ __ __

3. "Hey, wait a minute" man __ __ __ __ (__) __

4. NBA player, NFL coach   (__) __ __ __ __

5. Winningest college coach (__) __ __ __ __ __ __ __

6. AFL and NFL title winner __ __ __ (__) __ __

7. Penn State Patriarch   (__) __ __ __ __ __ __

8. "Air....."   __ __ __ __ (__) __ __

9. He punched Charlie   __ __ __ __ (__)
   Bauman

$\overline{}$ $\overline{}$ $\overline{}$ $\overline{}$ $\overline{}$ $\overline{}$ $\overline{}$ $\overline{}$ $\overline{}$

   1 2 3   4 5 6 7 8 9

1.   *Switzer.*

2.   *Halas.*

3.   *Madden.*

4.   *Grant.*

5.   *Robinson.*

6.   *Ewbank.*

7.   *Paterno.*

8.   *Coryell.*

9.   *Hayes.*

T H E   G R A P E S

TRIVIQUATIONS

Test your math and your football wits with this quiz. Fill in the number portion of the answers suggested by the clues and then perform the arithmetic to solve the Triviquation. Be sure to watch for fractions and signs.

1. $\dfrac{\text{Total NFL Teams}}{\begin{array}{c}\text{Head Coaches in}\\ \text{Cowboy History}\end{array}} \times \text{Bronco Amigos} - \text{Kickoff Spot} = \begin{array}{c}\text{Fordham Blocks}\\ \text{of Granite}\end{array}$

2. $\dfrac{\begin{array}{c}\text{Davis, Brown \& Little}\\ \text{Number at Syracuse}\end{array}}{\text{Fearsome Rams}} - \text{TD} + \dfrac{\text{Viking Super}}{\text{Bowl Wins}} = \text{AFC East Teams}$

3. $\dfrac{\text{Tom Dempsey's Record}}{\text{Field Goal}} - \dfrac{\text{Bobby Mitchell's}}{\text{Number}} = \dfrac{\text{Miami's Points in}}{\text{Super Bowl VII}}$

4. $\dfrac{\begin{array}{c}\text{K.C. Super}\\ \text{Bowl I Score}\end{array}}{\text{Safety}} \times \dfrac{\begin{array}{c}\text{Blanda}\\ \text{Retirement Age}\end{array}}{\text{Notre Dame Horsemen}} = \dfrac{\text{Chuck Bednarik's}}{\text{Number}}$

5. $\dfrac{\begin{array}{c}\text{Height of}\\ \text{Goalpost Crossbar}\end{array}}{\begin{array}{c}\text{NFC East Teams}\\ \text{West of Mississippi}\end{array}} \times \dfrac{\text{TDs by Rookie}}{\text{Gale Sayers}} = \dfrac{\text{Length of Canadian}}{\text{Football Field}}$

1. $\dfrac{28}{2} \times 3 - 35 = 7$

2. $\dfrac{44}{4} - 6 + 0 = 5$

3. $63 - 49 = 14$

4. $\dfrac{10}{2} \times \dfrac{48}{4} = 60$

5. $\dfrac{10}{2} \times 22 = 110$

GETTING THEIR KICKS

1. Name the kicker who's punted the ball the most times in pro football history.

2. The longest field goal in the NFL was a 63 yarder by Tom Dempsey of the New Orleans Saints against the Detroit Lions on November 8, 1970. Who was the holder?

3. Who kicked a 37 yard field goal to give Miami a 27-24 overtime playoff win against Kansas City in the longest game in NFL history?

4. St. Louis Cardinal placekicker Jim Baaken established an NFL record for most field goals in a game in 1962. How many?

5. Whose toe is enshrined in the Pro Football Hall of Fame?

6. Who holds the record for the longest return of a missed field goal?

7. George Blanda is tops on pro football's all-time scoring list with 2,002 points. Who's second?

8. Who kicked a 32 yard field goal with five seconds left to give the Colts a 16-13 win over the Cowboys in Super Bowl V?

9. Until 1976, no major-college placekicker had kicked a field goal beyond 63 yards, but in one game, a Texas A&M player booted a 64 and a 65 yarder to help the Aggies beat Baylor, 24-0. Name him.

10. Can you name the Arizona State placekicker who, from 1981 to 1984, scored 368 points to become major-college football's all-time leading scorer?

1.   *Dave Jennings, 1,154.*

2.   *Joe Scarpati.*

3.   *Garo Yepremian.*

4.   *Seven.*

5.   *Lou "The Toe" Groza's.*

6.   *Al Nelson of the Philadelphia Eagles, 101 yards, against Dallas, September 26, 1971.*

7.   *Jan Stenerud with 1,699 points.*

8.   *Jim O'Brien.*

9.   *Tony Franklin.*

10. *Luis Zendejas.*

PIGSKIN POTPOURRI

1. Bud Grant coached the Minnesota Vikings from 1967 to 1983. He was replaced by Les Steckel who lasted through only one season. Who replaced Steckel?

2. How many footballs does the home team supply for an NFL game?

3. Of the four major college bowl games — Cotton, Orange, Sugar and Rose — which one of the events is played in a facility also housing a professional football team?

4. Can you name the two Heisman trophy winners who also played major league baseball?

5. Who's the only player to rush for 1,000 yards in a single season in both the AFL and NFL?

6. What pro team would you find playing its home games near the junction of the Allegheny, Monogahela and Ohio Rivers?

7. What was the extra point attempt in the short lived WFL called?

8. Pete Rozelle's term as commissioner of the NFL lasted 29 years. Who was the man he replaced in 1960?

9. What two college teams play for The Little Brown Jug?

10. What Pennsylvania town was formerly called Mauch Chunk?

1.   *Bud Grant.*

2.   *24.*

3.   *The Sugar Bowl which is played in the Superdome, also home of the New Orleans Saints.*

4.   *Vic Janowicz and Bo Jackson.*

5.   *Mike Garrett.*

6.   *The Pittsburgh Steelers (at Three Rivers Stadium).*

7.   *The action point.*

8.   *Bert Bell.*

9.   *Michigan and Minnesota.*

10.   *Jim Thorpe, Pennsylvania.*

ON THE JOHN

Who are these "Johns?"

1. He was a Patriot standout guard from 1973-1985.

2. The number one pick of the Colts in the 1983 draft, he never played a down for them.

3. He was athletic director of New York's Downtown Athletic Club until 1936.

4. He holds the NFL mark for touchdowns in a season (24).

5. A defensive back for the 1958 and 1959 championship Colt teams, he was also a member of the Super Bowl-winning Jets in 1969.

6. Narrator of NFL films, he was known as the "Voice of God."

7. Baltimore tight end in the Sixties.

8. Notre Dame quarterback, he won the Heisman in 1964.

9. The Tooz . . .

10. Packer who scored the most points in a Pro Bowl (18).

1. *John Hannah.*

2. *John Elway.*

3. *John W. Heisman (as in the trophy).*

4. *John Riggins.*

5. *Johnny Sample.*

6. *John Facenda.*

7. *John Mackey.*

8. *John Huarte.*

9. *John Matuszak.*

10. *John Brockington.*

Thoughts of the Throne

Carroll Rosenbloom, then the owner of the Baltimore Colts, was the first to give 33-year-old Pete Rozelle the news that the NFL had elected him as its commissioner. The date - January 26, 1960. The place - the men's room of a Miami Beach hotel (Rozelle was washing his hands at the time.).

Heady Questions— AFC

What's wrong with each of these helmets?

1.

COLTS

2.

BRONCOS

3.

RAIDERS

4.

PATRIOTS

5.

STEELERS

6.

DOLPHINS

Here are the AFC Helmets as they should appear.

1. *Hoof was upside down.*

2. *Bronco was missing.*

3. *The eye patch has been removed.*

4. *Ball was missing.*

5. *The word "Steelers" was eliminated.*

6. *The "M" was absent.*

Heady Questions— NFC

How have these helmets been altered?

1.

RAMS

2.

REDSKINS

3.

BUCS

4.

SAINTS

5.

FALCONS

6.

COWBOYS

The NFC helmets are shown accurately below.

1. The buffalo — as in Buffalo Bills — should not appear on the Rams helmet.

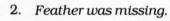

2. Feather was missing.

3. Knife in Buc's mouth was removed.

4. "Saints" name should not appear on helmet.

5. Falcon was flying in wrong direction.

6. Cowboys' logo is a star, not a horse.

FIRST OF ALL

1. Who was the first winner of the Heisman Trophy?

2. Name the quarterback and the receiver who combined for the first Super Bowl touchdown.

3. Who was the first draft selection in Atlanta Falcons' history?

4. What was the first pro football team to have emblems on their helmets?

5. Who was the first soccer-style kicker in pro football? Hint: He began his career with the Buffalo Bills in 1964.

6. The Houston Oilers and Los Angeles Chargers played in the first AFL Championship game, January 1, 1961. Who won?

7. When the Seattle Seahawks began play in the NFL in 1976, who was their head coach?

8. Who was the first player in major-college history to rush for 1,000 or more yards in all four of his varsity years?

9. What NFL team was the first to play its home games in a domed stadium?

10. Instant replay was first used as an officiating aid in:
    a) 1964
    b) 1974
    c) 1986
    d) 1988.

1.   *Jay Berwanger.*

2.   *Green Bay's Bart Starr threw a 37 yard touchdown pass to Max McGee.*

3.   *Tommy Nobis, 1966.*

4.   *The Los Angeles Rams. Halfback Fred Gehrke, an art major in college, painted horns on their helmets in 1948.*

5.   *Pete Gogolak.*

6.   *The Oilers, 24-16.*

7.   *Jack Patera.*

8.   *Tony Dorsett.*

9.   *Houston, 1968.*

10. *C.*

DATELINES

We've provided the dateline. You come up with the headline.

1. Dallas, Texas — February 25, 1989

2. Carlisle, Pennsylvania — March 28, 1953

3. Baltimore, Maryland — March 29, 1984

4. Los Angeles, California — January 15, 1967

5. Canton, Ohio — September 7, 1963

6. New Brunswick, New Jersey — November 6, 1869

7. New York, New York — December 28, 1958

8. Washington, D.C. — December 8, 1940

9. Boston, Massachusetts — September 9, 1960

10. Cleveland, Ohio — September 21, 1970

1.   *Cowboys Fire 28 Year Head Coach Tom Landry*

2.   *Hometown Hero Jim Thorpe Dies*

3.   *Colts' Owner Irsay Moves Team to Indianapolis*

4.   *Packers Beat Chiefs in Super Bowl I*

5.   *Pro Football Hall of Fame Opens*

6.   *First College Football Game Sees Rutgers Defeat Princeton, 6-4*

7.   *Colts Win NFL Championship Against Giants in Overtime*

8.   *Bears Hand Redskins NFL's Biggest Thrashing — 73 - 0 — in Championship Game*

9.   *Broncos 13, Patriots 10 in AFL's First Regular Season Game*

10.   *Browns Top Jets in Monday Night Football Inaugural*

CONFERENCE CALL

Match the team with its college athletic conference.

1.	UCLA	a.	Atlantic Coast Conference
2.	Alabama	b.	Big 8
3.	Iowa State	c.	Big 10
4.	Baylor	d.	Ivy League
5.	Clemson	e.	Mid-American Conference
6.	Princeton	f.	Pacific Coast Athletic Association
7.	Air Force	g.	Pac 10
8.	Bowling Green	h.	Southeastern Conference
9.	San Jose State	i.	Southwest Conference
10.	Purdue	j.	Western Athletic Conference

1.   G.

2.   H.

3.   B.

4.   I.

5.   A.

6.   D.

7.   J.

8.   E.

9.   F.

10.   C.

Thoughts of the Throne

From Toilet Bowl to Super Bowl — Joe Namath was signed to a pro contract in a hotel bathroom. As the story goes, Namath, Sonny Werblin (president of the Jets at the time), and attorneys were present in a hotel room. While the lawyers were bickering over contract details, Namath headed for the bathroom and motioned for Werblin to follow him. Behind closed door, Namath asked Werblin if he had another copy of the contract. Werblin did, Namath signed it and the rest is history.

QUOTE UNQUOTE

Using the answers suggested by the clues below (HINT: They are all receivers.), fill in the letters which correspond with the numbers at the bottom of the page to complete the following statement. When legendary Hall of Fame quarterback Sammy Baugh was ordered by Redskins coach Ray Flaherty to "Hit the end in the eye with the ball," this was his response:

1. Caught more Super Bowl passes than anyone.

    _ _ _ _ _ (_) _ _ _

2. Redskin Hall of Fame receiver.

    _ (_) _ _ _ _ _ _ _ _ _ _ _

3. #80 out of Mississippi Valley State.

    _ _ _ _ _ _ (_) _ _

4. Oiler who caught 101 in '64.

    (_) _ _ _ _ _ _ _ _ _ _ _ _ _ _

5. Eagle who caught passes in 127 straight games.

    _ _ _ _ _ _ _ _ _ _ _ _(_) _ _ _

6. Won Olympic gold, played in Cowboy silver.

    _ _ _ _ _ _ (_) _

7. Colt turned coach.

    _ _ (_) _ _ _ _ _ _ _ _ _

8. All-time pass receiving leader.

    _ _ _ _ _ _ _ _ _ (_) _ _

    $\overline{}\,\overline{}\,\overline{}\,\overline{}\,\overline{}\,\overline{}\,\overline{}\,\overline{}$?
    1 2 3 4 5   6 7 8

1.   *Lynn Swann.*

2.   *Charley Taylor.*

3.   *Jerry Rice.*

4.   *Charley Hennigan.*

5.   *Harold Carmichael.*

6.   *Bob Hayes.*

7.   *Raymond Berry.*

8.   *Steve Largent.*

<u>W</u> <u>h</u> <u>i</u> <u>c</u> <u>h</u>   <u>e</u> <u>y</u> <u>e</u>?

Thoughts of the Throne

"I'm the only coach in history to go straight from the White House to the outhouse."
Former Georgia Tech football coach Pepper Rodgers
who was fired the day after he had lunch
with President Jimmy Carter

PIGSKIN POTPOURRI

1. What player had a career spanning four decades?

2. What trophy does the Super Bowl winner get?

3. Whose statue is outside the Pro Football Hall of Fame?

4. Do you know the first college to win three consecutive Orange Bowls?

5. Who kicked 23 consecutive NFL field goals?

6. Name the football player who appeared on President Nixon's "enemy" list.

7. In what city is the Army-Navy game played?

8. How high are the bars which extend upward from the crossbar in the NFL?

9. What referee is responsible for timing the game?

10. Who was made commissioner of the American Football League in 1959?

1.   *George Blanda.*

2.   *The Vince Lombardi Trophy.*

3.   *Jim Thorpe's.*

4.   *Nebraska.*

5.   *Mark Moseley.*

6.   *Joe Namath.*

7.   *Philadelphia.*

8.   *Thirty feet.*

9.   *The line judge.*

10. *Joe Foss.*

BY THE NUMBERS

1. What is the distance between the uprights on a pro football goal post?

2. Former Notre Dame quarterback Joe Montana wore what single digit number?

3. How many domed stadiums are there in the NFL?

4. Ernie Davis died of leukemia before getting a chance to play for the Browns. Cleveland retired a jersey number in his honor. What number was that?

5. How many feet wide is a football field?

6. How wide is the white sideline in the NFL?

7. What number did Gerald Ford wear when he played center for Michigan?

8. Walter Payton holds the NFL record for yards gained rushing in one game. How many?

9. The Redskins and Giants played the highest scoring game in NFL history in 1966. What was the outcome?

10. Johnny Unitas' consecutive game touchdown pass record stands at what number?

1.   *18 feet, 6 inches.*

2.   *3.*

3.   *6.*

4.   *45.*

5.   *160.*

6.   *6 feet.*

7.   *48.*

8.   *275.*

9.   *Redskins 72, Giants 41.*

10. *47.*

THREE ON A MATCH

Match the players, all first round draft picks, with their college and with the pro team which selected them.

Player	College	Pro Team
Bo Jackson	1) USC	a) Tampa Bay
John Elway	2) Notre Dame	b) Buffalo
O.J. Simpson	3) Auburn	c) L.A. Rams
Billy Sims	4) Vanderbilt	d) Atlanta
Irving Fryar	5) Oklahoma	e) New England
Paul Hornung	6) Pennsylvania	f) Dallas
Bill Wade	7) Tennessee State	g) Baltimore
Steve Bartkowski	8) California	h) Green Bay
Chuck Bednarik	9) Stanford	i) Philadelphia
Ed Jones	10) Nebraska	j) Detroit

Bo Jackson, 3 and a.

John Elway, 9 and g.

O.J. Simpson, 1 and b.

Billy Sims, 5 and j.

Irving Fryar, 10 and e.

Paul Hornung, 2 and h.

Bill Wade, 4 and c.

Steve Bartkowski, 8 and d.

Chuck Bednarik, 6 and i.

Ed Jones, 7 and f.

THE SUPER BOWL

1. Who has scored the most touchdowns in Super Bowl history?

2. Name the only man to play in a major league baseball game and a Super Bowl game.

3. What two teams have been to the Super Bowl the most?

4. Who coined the term "Super Bowl?"

5. Who is the winningest Super Bowl coach?

6. In what state has the most Super Bowls been played?

7. Ten NFL teams have never been to the big game. How many can you name?

8. Which two stadiums have hosted both a Super Bowl and a World Series game?

9. The MVPs for Super Bowls X and XI were both wide receivers. Who were they?

10. What team scored the most points in a Super Bowl game?

1. *Franco Harris, 4.*

2. *Tom Brown (for the baseball Senators and football Packers).*

3. *Dallas and Miami (each have a record of 2 and 3).*

4. *K.C. Chiefs owner Lamar Hunt.*

5. *Chuck Noll (4 wins, no defeats).*

6. *California, 8.*

7. *The Bills, Browns, Oilers, Chargers, Seahawks, Cardinals, Lions, Buccaneers, Falcons, and Saints.*

8. *San Diego's Jack Murphy Stadium and the Los Angeles Memorial Coliseum.*

9. *Lynn Swann and Fred Biletnikoff.*

10. *The Chicago Bears, 46 (against New England in 1986).*

LOOKING FOR A LOSER

The Dallas Cowboys and New England Patriots are two of three clubs which hold the NFL mark for losing the most games in a season. Do you know the other team which shares the record? If not, you can narrow it down with the word search below. Twenty-seven of the twenty-eight NFL teams are listed. The club in question has been left out. Teams can be found horizontally, vertically, and diagonally but always in a straight line.

```
B  L  I  O  N  S  R  E  G  R  A  H  C
R  O  S  T  C  A  R  D  I  N  A  L  S
B  E  N  G  A  L  S  R  S  X  S  T  T
Y  U  C  O  W  B  O  Y  S  R  E  S  L
P  A  C  K  E  R  S  E  E  E  A  F  O
A  S  B  C  S  M  L  N  L  D  H  E  C
T  T  I  C  A  G  I  E  N  S  A  I  B
R  N  L  R  A  N  R  Q  R  K  W  H  R
I  A  L  E  Y  S  E  E  J  I  K  C  O
O  I  S  T  E  J  L  E  U  N  S  V  W
T  G  R  R  A  I  D  E  R  S  M  F  N
S  O  C  N  O  R  B  P  O  S  A  G  S
F  A  L  C  O  N  S  G  N  I  K  I  V
G  I  A  D  O  L  P  H  I  N  S  H  W
```

For your reference, here's a checklist of all twenty-eight teams.

Bills	Oilers	Cowboys	Packers
Colts	Steelers	Giants	Vikings
Dolphins	Broncos	Eagles	Buccaneers
Patriots	Chiefs	Cardinals	Falcons
Jets	Raiders	Redskins	Rams
Bengals	Chargers	Bears	Saints
Browns	Seahawks	Lions	Forty-Niners

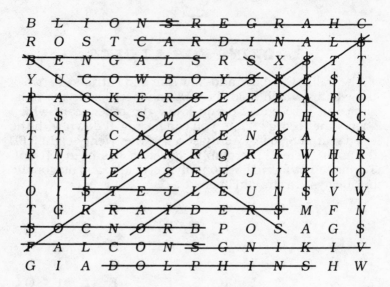

And the answer is... The New Orleans Saints who were one and fifteen in 1980.

Thoughts of the Throne

Way back when, Georgia Tech coach John Heisman (yes, *the* Heisman) refused to allow his players to take hot water baths or use soap during the week before a game because, as he said, they were "debilitating."

TRIVIQUATIONS

Here's some more math for the football chalkboard. See quiz 21 if you've forgotten the instructions.

1. $\dfrac{\text{Year AFL Began Play}}{\text{Pete Gent Book "North Dallas _____"}} \div \dfrac{\text{Notre Dame Mules}}{\text{Super Bowls Played in Michigan}} = \dfrac{\text{NFL Mammal Team Nicknames}}{}$

2. $\text{Domed Stadiums in NFL} \times \dfrac{\text{Illegal Motion Penalty}}{} = \dfrac{\text{Footage From Goal line to Goal line}}{\text{Tarkenton Number}}$

3. $\dfrac{\text{Ivy League Schools}}{\text{Griffin Heismans}} + \text{Tom Harmon's famous "Old _____"} = \dfrac{\text{Amos Alonzo Stagg's Ripe Old Age}}{}$

4. $\dfrac{\text{Games in an NFL Regular Season}}{\text{Seasons Jim Brown Led NFL in Rushing}} \times \dfrac{\text{Fears' Catches in One Game}}{\text{Field Goal}} = \dfrac{\text{Number Worn by Winning QB in 9 Straight Super Bowls}}{}$

5. $\dfrac{\text{Riggins Single Season TD Record}}{\text{Dorsett's Longest Run}} - \dfrac{\text{AFC Central Teams}}{\text{O'Neal's Record Punt}} = \dfrac{\text{Super Bowl Won by Bears}}{}$

1. $$\frac{1960}{40} \div \frac{7}{1} = 7$$

2. $$6 \times 5 = \frac{300}{10}$$

3. $$\frac{8}{2} + 98 = 102$$

4. $$\frac{16}{8} \times \frac{18}{3} = 12$$

5. $$\frac{24 - 4}{99 - 98} = 20$$

Thoughts of the Throne

Name the defensive back who was selected MVP of the 1973 Super Bowl when the Dolphins beat the Redskins 14-7 to go undefeated at 17-0 for the season.
Hint: Think toilet paper brands.

Jake Scott.

PIGSKIN POTPOURRI

1. Who was Notre Dame playing when Knute Rockne urged his squad to "win one for the Gipper?"

2. Who manufactures NFL footballs?

3. Where was the Gotham Bowl played?

4. Who coached the Bears before Mike Ditka?

5. What would you find at 2121 George Halas Drive N.W.?

6. Is it the visiting or the home team that gets to call the coin toss?

7. In the 1965 season, both Baltimore quarterbacks, Johnny Unitas and Gary Cuozzo, were injured and the Colts were forced to go with a running back at that position for the last four games that year. Who was he?

8. His real name is O.A. Phillips but you can call him Bum. Do you know, though, what his initials stand for?

9. Which three AFC teams were part of the NFL before the two leagues merged?

10. Who was the last man to score six touchdowns in an NFL game?

1.   *Army (Notre Dame won, 12-6).*

2.   *Wilson.*

3.   *New York City.*

4.   *Neill Armstrong.*

5.   *The Pro Football Hall of Fame.*

6.   *The visitors.*

7.   *Tom Matte.*

8.   *Oail Andrew.*

9.   *The Colts, Browns and Steelers.*

10.   *Gale Sayers (1965).*

MULTIPLE CHOICE

1. Five men were selected ahead of Jim Brown in the 1957 NFL draft. They were Paul Hornung, Len Dawson, Ron Kramer, Jon Arnett and: a) Alex Karras   b) John Brodie   c) Bart Starr   d) Frank Gifford.

2. The only NFL team which has not won a playoff game is: a) Buffalo   b) Detroit   c)New Orleans   d) Tampa Bay.

3. Len Dawson holds the record for most fumbles in a game with: a) 4   b) 5   c) 6   d) 7.

4. The quarterback who holds career NFL records for most passes, completions, most yardage and most touchdown passes is: a) Fran Tarkenton   b) Johnny Unitas   c) Dan Fouts   d) Joe Montana.

5. Who scored the most points in a single season? a) Lou Groza   b) Pat Summerall   c) Gale Sayers   d) Paul Hornung.

6. The first man who played solely in the AFL to be elected to the NFL Hall of Fame is: a) Ron Mix   b) Keith Lincoln   c) Don Maynard   d) Tobin Rote.

7. The first draft choice in USFL history was: a) Herschel Walker   b) Steve Young   c) Dan Marino   d) Keith Byars.

8. Which one of these sportscasters has not appeared on *Monday Night Football?* a) Alex Karras   b) Jim Lampley   c) Keith Jackson   d) Fred Williamson.

9. Which one of these football players did not play major league baseball? a) Jim Thorpe   b) George Halas   c) Don Hutson   d) Ernie Nevers.

10. In 1942, the Rose Bowl was played in: a) Pasadena, California   b) Las Vegas, Nevada   c) Denver, Colorado   d) Durham, North Carolina.

1.   *B.*

2.   *C.*

3.   *D.*

4.   *A.*

5.   *D, 176.*

6.   *A.*

7.   *C.*

8.   *B.*

9.   *C.*

10.   *D. Because of military conditions during World War II, the U.S. did not want large crowd gatherings on the west coast. The game was moved to Durham, the only time the contest was not played in Pasadena, where Duke was upset by Oregon State, 20-16.*

BABY BOOMERS QUIZ

How well do you remember the Sixties?

1. The AFL began play in 1960 with eight teams: the Boston Patriots, Buffalo Bills, Dallas Texans, Denver Broncos, Houston Oilers, Los Angeles Chargers, New York Titans and Oakland Raiders. Do you know who any of the head coaches were?

2. What team won the NCAA Championship three times in the Sixties?

3. In 1964, a Minnesota Vikings defensive end picked up a San Francisco 49er's fumble and raced 60 yards — the wrong way for a safety. Can you name him?

4. What collegiate team did Tom Cahill coach?

5. What team won the most Super Bowls in the Sixties?

6. Name the two players Pete Rozelle suspended for gambling in 1963.

7. The NFL was realigned from 1967 to 1969. There were four divisions. The Eastern Conference had the Capitol and Century Divisions. What were the two Western Conference divisions called?

8. The first combined AFL-NFL draft took place in 1967. Do you know the Michigan State player who was the top pick?

9. The Green Bay Packers and Kansas City Chiefs participated in the first Super Bowl. In their respective league championships, what teams did they beat to make it to the big one?

10. A widely circulated incorrect trivia question about 1963 goes like this: The MVPs of the NFL, the AFL, and the American and National Leagues in baseball all wore the number 32. Who were they? The fact is that, yes, Jim Brown of the NFL, Elston Howard of the American League and Sandy Koufax of the National League were MVPs in '63 and did wear 32; however, the AFL winner did not wear that number. Who was he and what was his number?

1. *Lou Saban, Patriots; Buster Ramsey, Bills; Hank Stram, Texans; Frankie Filchock, Broncos; Lou Rymkus, Oilers; Sid Gillman, Chargers; Sammy Baugh, Titans; Eddie Erdelatz, Raiders.*

2. *Alabama.*

3. *Jim Marshall.*

4. *Army.*

5. *Green Bay, 2.*

6. *Paul Hornung and Alex Karras.*

7. *Central and Coastal.*

8. *Defensive end Bubba Smith.*

9. *Kansas City topped Buffalo while Green Bay defeated Dallas. The Packers took the Super Bowl, 35-10.*

10. *Clem Daniels of the Oakland Raiders, number 36.*

40

SIGN LANGUAGE

What's the ref signalling?

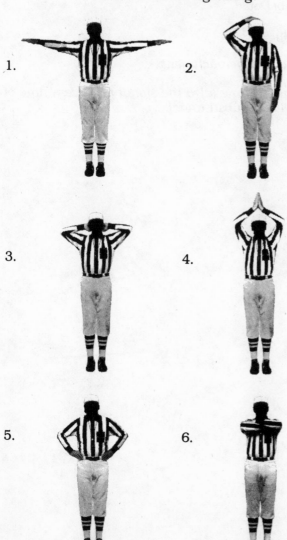

1.

2.

3.

4.

5.

6.

1.   *Unsportsmanlike Conduct.*

2.   *Ineligible Receiver (or ineligible kicking team member downfield).*

3.   *Loss of Down.*

4.   *Safety.*

5.   *Offside or Encroachment.*

6.   *Delay of Game (also the signal for excess time out and illegal substitution).*

FOUR-LETTER MEN

The answers to these clues are all four-letter last names.

1. A former Giant defensive back, he was a 1964 Olympic gold medalist.

2. Alphabetically, you'd find him in the back of football's telephone book.

3. AFL founding father.

4. The Super Bowl has been a four ring circus for this coach.

5. He was the first Buc to gain a thousand yards.

6. Giant-Redskin Hall of Fame linebacker.

7. A 50's and 60's Lions defensive back, could he have been an Eli grad?

8. A defensive end, he was Super Bowl XX's MVP.

9. A quarterback for the AFL, he later became the signal caller for HUD.

10. The only quarterback to play in a CFL championship and in a Super Bowl game.

1. *Henry Carr.*

2. *Jim Zorn.*

3. *Lamar Hunt.*

4. *Chuck Noll.*

5. *Ricky Bell.*

6. *Sam Huff.*

7. *Yale Lary.*

8. *Richard Dent.*

9. *Jack Kemp (director of Housing and Urban Development).*

10. *Joe Kapp.*

BOWL GAMES

Match the bowl game with its site.

1.	Cotton	a.	Houston, TX
2.	Orange	b.	Dallas, TX
3.	Rose	c.	Miami, FL
4.	Sugar	d.	Jacksonville, FL
5.	Bluebonnet	e.	El Paso, TX
6.	Fiesta	f.	Tempe, AZ
7.	Citrus	g.	Pasadena, CA
8.	Gator	h.	Memphis, TN
9.	Liberty	i.	Orlando, FL
10.	Sun	j.	New Orleans, LA

1. *B.*

2. *C.*

3. *G.*

4. *J.*

5. *A.*

6. *F.*

7. *I.*

8. *D.*

9. *H.*

10. *E.*

PIGSKIN POTPOURRI

1. What is the emblem on a New Orleans Saints helmet called?

2. Who is the "Father of American Football?"

3. What football player has appeared on a U.S. postage stamp?

4. What position did George Gipp play for Notre Dame?

5. Who was the first draft pick in Dallas Cowboys history?

6. The Big Ten and Pac-10 champs play in what bowl game?

7. The Giants and Bears are two of six teams undefeated in Super Bowl competition. How many of the others can you name?

8. During Jim Brown's nine year career, he led the league in rushing eight times. Who won the rushing crown the only other season?

9. When you see a flag on the play, it's a bright gold one. What color were NFL officials' flags until 1965?

10. The first two Heisman Trophy winners to make the Pro Football Hall of Fame did so in 1985. Who were they?

1.   *A fleur-de-lis.*

2.   *Walter Camp.*

3.   *Jim Thorpe.*

4.   *Halfback.*

5.   *Bob Lilly.*

6.   *The Rose Bowl.*

7.   *The Steelers, 49ers, Packers and Jets.*

8.   *Jim Taylor.*

9.   *White.*

10.   *O.J. Simpson and Roger Staubach.*

MINDING YOUR P's AND Q's

The names below contain p's and q's which have already been noted. Using the clues given, fill in the blanks.

1. _ _ _ _ Q _ _ _ _
   Receiver who's earned his wings.

2. _ _ _ _ _ _ _ _ Q _ _ _ _
   Former Steeler punter.

3. _ _ _ _ P _ _ _ _
   A purple people eater.

4. _ _ _ _ _ P _ _ _
   First 2,000 yard man.

5. _ _ _ _ _ _ P P _ _ _ _ _ _ _
   AFL all-time leading scorer.

6. _ _ _ _ _ _ P _ _ _ _ _
   Big Daddy.

7. _ _ _ _ _ _ Q _ _
   Frenchy the running back.

8. Q _ _ _ _ _ _ _ _ _ _ _
   NBA player drafted by Redskins in 1976.

9. _ _ _ _ _ _ P _ _
   He was born Mark Kirby Dupas.

10. _ _ _ _ _ P _ _ _ _
    Lone Raider to appear in Super Bowls II, XI, and XV.

1. *Mike Quick.*

2. *Craig Colquitt.*

3. *Alan Page.*

4. *O.J. Simpson.*

5. *Gino Cappelletti.*

6. *Gene Lipscomb.*

7. *John Fuqua.*

8. *Quinn Buckner.*

9. *Mark Duper.*

10. *Gene Upshaw.*

Thoughts of the Throne

"Whether it's politics or football, winning is like shaving:
You do it every day or you wind up looking like a bum."
Jack Kemp

WHO AM I?

1.   I retired when I was only 29 as I decided to go from an eleven man team to "The Dirty Dozen."

2.   I played college ball at Tennessee State and was the first pick in the 1974 draft. I earned All-Pro honors in the NFL but gave up football for boxing. When that proved too tall a task, I returned to the gridiron to finish my sporting career.

3.   My sack dance showed that I was never camera shy, but Nielsen problems caused premature retirement.

4.   A Rhodes scholar, I led the NFL in rushing two out of the three years I played and then was put on the bench.

5.   I was an All-American at Syracuse and was drafted by the pros, but preferred calling balls and strikes to blocking tackles and linebackers.

6.   "Rocky" was the word for my career. I spent two seasons in pro football as a linebacker for the Oakland Raiders but have enjoyed more success on Hollywood than highlight films.

7.   My brother and I were both linemen and teammates. My fearsome play — no Father Murphy was I — earned me a spot in the Hall of Fame.

8.   I caught a touchdown pass from Y.A. Tittle. To shed some more light on my situation, I also hit a homerun off of Sandy Koufax.

9.   Most of my NFL career was spent with the Chicago Bears but I did play with the 1927 New York Yankees. School days were my red-letter days, though, when I made number 77 famous at the University of Illinois.

10.   I was a Heisman Trophy winner whose pro debut was a royal one. I averaged 6.8 yards per carry in my rookie year.

1. *Jim Brown.*

2. *Ed "Too Tall" Jones.*

3. *Mark Gastineau who left the Jets in midseason of 1988 because girlfriend Brigitte Nielsen was ill.*

4. *U.S. Supreme Court Justice Byron "Whizzer" White.*

5. *Ron Luciano.*

6. *Carl Weathers who played Apollo Creed in the "Rocky" movies as well as the title role in "Action Jackson."*

7. *Merlin Olsen.*

8. *Alvin Dark, former major league baseball player and football player at Louisiana State (where he caught Tittle's TD pass).*

9. *Red Grange. Incidentally, it was on the 1927 football New York Yankees where Grange played.*

10. *Bo Jackson.*

THROUGH THE EIGHTIES

1. The Steelers became the first team to win four Super Bowls when they captured Super Bowl XIV on January 20, 1980. Who did they beat?

2. What USC running back set a major college rushing record in 1981 racking up 2,342 yards?

3. The NFL now has a 16 game regular season schedule. How many games did each team play in 1982?

4. The 1983 winners of the Heisman Trophy and the Outland Trophy were Mike Rozier and Dean Steinkuhler, respectively, marking only the fourth time that both winners came from the same college. What school were they from?

5. 1984 was a season for NFL records. Can you name the quarterback who threw 48 touchdown passes, the receiver who caught 106 passes and the running back who gained 2,105 yards?

6. He quarterbacked the first AFL team to win a Super Bowl and in 1985 he made Pro Football's Hall of Fame. Name him.

7. What TV show became the longest-running prime-time series in the history of the ABC network in 1986?

8. He led the league in scoring with 138 points and was *The Sporting News* NFL Player of the Year in 1987. Who?

9. Little did he know that it would be his last opening day appearance, but when Tom Landry was on the sideline in 1988 it was his 29th consecutive opening day as head coach of the Dallas Cowboys. That tied a record held by what other coach?

10. In 1989, Pete Rozelle resigned as NFL Commissioner. What is Rozelle's first name?

1. *The Rams, 31-19.*

2. *Marcus Allen.*

3. *Nine. It was a strike-shortened season.*

4. *Nebraska.*

5. *Dan Marino, Art Monk, and Eric Dickerson, in that order.*

6. Joe Namath.

7. Monday Night Football.

8. *Jerry Rice.*

9. *Curly Lambeau.*

10. *Alvin.*

STADIA-MANIA

1. What is the oldest stadium in the NFL?

2. What four stadiums did the New York Giants call home during the 1970s?

3. Name the football stadium with the largest seating capacity in the U.S.

4. Where did the Dallas Cowboys play their first home games?

5. What were Denver's Mile High Stadium and Green Bay's Lambeau Field formerly called?

6. What NFL stadium is located at 1200 Featherstone Road?

7. Name the Houston stadium that was the site of Super Bowl VIII when the Dolphins topped the Vikings, 24-7.

8. Another Houston stadium was the scene of the first AFL title game won by the Oilers, 24-16, over the L.A. Chargers. Name it.

9. The NFL Pro Bowl is played annually at what stadium?

10. The first NFL Pro Bowl game was played in 1939 in Los Angeles at: a) Chavez Ravine b) Memorial Coliseum c) Wrigley Field d) Sally Field.

1. *Chicago's Soldier Field.*

2. *Yankee Stadium, The Yale Bowl, Shea Stadium, and Giants Stadium.*

3. *The Rose Bowl (105,000).*

4. *The Cotton Bowl.*

5. *Bears Stadium and City Stadium, respectively.*

6. *The Pontiac Silverdome (home of the Detroit Lions).*

7. *Rice Stadium.*

8. *Jeppeson Stadium (a high school field).*

9. *Aloha Stadium in Honolulu.*

10. *C (Wrigley Field was a park used primarily for minor league baseball, but in this instance hosted the inaugural Pro Bowl.)*

YOU MAKE THE CALL

Test your knowledge of football's rules with these hypothetical situations.

1.   The 49ers line up for a point after touchdown against the Browns. Joe Montana holds. The ball is snapped. Montana fumbles, picks it up and throws a desperation pass which is intercepted by Frank Minnifield who returns it for a touchdown. Or is it?

2.   Bills quarterback Jim Kelly fades back deep into his own end zone. Running back Robb Riddick attempts to give Kelly pass protection but clips an opposing lineman. Kelly then throws an incompletion. The official rules loss of down and a penalty half the distance to the Bills' own goal line. Was the ref right?

3.   The Dolphins have just suffered a safety against the Bengals. Miami elects to punt from its 20 yard line on the ensuing free kick. The ball travels just 12 yards and a Dolphin player recovers it giving Miami the ball first and ten. Is this "onside punt" allowed?

4.   Phil Simms throws a pass which is deflected off an official and then caught by Giants tight end Mark Bavaro. Is the catch legal?

5.   Philadelphia defensive end Reggie White is driven out of bounds by a Dallas opposing lineman. As Cowboy running back Herschel Walker is about to turn the corner and race down the sideline, White recovers, steps back in bounds and makes the tackle. Can White do that?

1.   No. The defensive team can never score on an extra point attempt. As soon as the defense gets possession, or a kick is blocked, the ball is dead.

2.   The official goofed on this one. When the offensive team commits an infraction behind its own goal line, it's a safety.

3.   Yes. And this actually happened in a Miami-Cincinnati game in 1980.

4.   Yes.

5.   Yes. It is legal for a defensive player, at any time, to step out of bounds and then back in to make a tackle.

PIGSKIN POTPOURRI

1. Quarterback Jim McMahon was traded by Chicago to San Diego in 1989 leaving him 30 completions shy of the Bears' passing record which is held by whom?

2. What city has hosted the most Super Bowls?

3. Who was the leading rusher in AFL history?

4. Which is deeper, a National Football League or a Canadian Football League end zone?

5. Two receivers have caught five touchdown passes in a game. One is Bob Shaw of the Chicago Cardinals. Who is the other?

6. How long is a high school football game?

7. What two men swapped NFL teams in 1972?

8. Name the running back who set a major college scoring record of 43 points in his final collegiate game.

9. Does a football weigh more or less than a pound?

10. In 1976, two new teams became part of the NFL. Do you know them?

Answers

1. *Sid Luckman (904 completions).*

2. *New Orleans, 7.*

3. *Clem Daniels, 5,101 yards.*

4. *A CFL end zone is 25 yards deep, 15 more than the NFL's.*

5. *Kellen Winslow of the San Diego Chargers.*

6. *48 minutes.*

7. *Carroll Rosenbloom traded the Colts for Robert Irsay's Rams.*

8. *Jim Brown of Syracuse.*

9. *Less (14 to 15 ounces).*

10. *The Tampa Bay Buccaneers and the Seattle Seahawks.*

LAST CALL

With what team did each of these hall of famers wind up their careers?

1. Herb Adderley

2. Joe Namath

3. Johnny Unitas

4. O.J. Simpson

5. Lance Alworth

6. Mike Ditka

7. John Henry Johnson

8. Don Maynard

9. Jim Taylor

10. Forrest Gregg

1.   *Cowboys.*

2.   *Rams.*

3.   *Chargers.*

4.   *49ers.*

5.   *Cowboys.*

6.   *Cowboys.*

7.   *Oilers.*

8.   *Cardinals.*

9.   *Saints.*

10.   *Cowboys.*

The Bathroom Library

THE BATHROOM BASKETBALL BOOK
THE BATHROOM GUEST BOOK
THE BATHROOM CROSSWORD PUZZLE BOOK
THE BATHROOM DIGEST
THE BATHROOM TRIVIA BOOK
THE BATHROOM ENTERTAINMENT BOOK
THE BATHROOM SPORTS QUIZ BOOK
THE BATHROOM SPORTS QUOTE BOOK
THE BATHROOM GAME BOOK
THE BATHROOM BASEBALL BOOK
THE BATHROOM FOOTBALL BOOK
THE BATHROOM GOLF BOOK
THE BATHROOM SOAP OPERA BOOK
THE BATHROOM INSPIRATION BOOK

For further information, write to:
Red-Letter Press, Inc.
P.O. Box 393,
Saddle River, N.J. 07458